Frederick North

A Letter to the Right Honourable Lord North

On the East-India bill now depending in Parliament

Frederick North

A Letter to the Right Honourable Lord North
On the East-India bill now depending in Parliament

ISBN/EAN: 9783337195724

Printed in Europe, USA, Canada, Australia, Japan

Cover: Foto ©Suzi / pixelio.de

More available books at **www.hansebooks.com**

A

LETTER

TO THE

RIGHT HONOURABLE

LORD NORTH;

ON THE

EAST-INDIA BILL

NOW DEPENDING IN

PARLIAMENT.

LONDON:

Printed for J. ALMON, in *Piccadilly*; and
BROTHERTON and SEWELL, in *Cornhill*.

MDCCLXXII.

(Price One Shilling.)

ADVERTISEMENT.

THAT thofe attentive to India matters are put to any kind of expence for a perufal of the following hafty performance, fuch as it may be thought, has been contrary to the inclination of its Author.

Having determined to fubmit fome ftrictures on the Eaft-India Bill, now depending in Parliament, to the confideration of all who may be interefted therein, the Writer of the following pages carried the part of it firft written to the Printer of the PUBLIC ADVERTISER; where, after making himfelf known, he left it, if approved, for infertion in that paper.

About two days after, on a Wednefday, he faw it inferted, with a notice at the end, that the publication would be continued. Upon which he immediately carried another nearly-equal part, and was then informed, that Friday and Monday would be the other days of publication.

A fecond and a third part accordingly appeared, each with a notice at the end of its intended continuation. But the fourth part not appearing on the day it fhould have done, the Writer went to the Printer's to enquire the caufe thereof; who, immediately on his appearance, had the manufcript returned to him by a Clerk, with this excufe; that Mr. WOODFALL had promifed to fpare one column of his paper for that purpofe, but could not fpare two. Nothing farther paffed thereon. The inftant delivery back of his papers, on the Writer's appearance, the cool civility fhewn in doing it, and the infufficiency of the excufe, all ferved to convince him, that fome new motive muft have occa-

fioned

fioned fo extraordinary a treatment, for the following reafons :

Firft, That no mention had ever before been made to him of either one or two columns.

Secondly, That all the three numbers publifhed, though not exactly of a length, had much exceeded one column, but neither had filled two.

Thirdly, That the manufcript pages of the fourth part were in number the fame as the other three which had been printed.

Fourthly, That it had not been unufual to infert letters of more than two columns in that paper, even on fubjects very little interefting to the public.

Fifthly, That the fame notice had been fubjoined to the third part of the letter as to the former two, that the publication would *be continued*.

Sixthly, That to the very fourth number of the manufcript, fo returned, the following notice was actually prefixed by the Writer ; *To be concluded in* our Friday's paper : and,

Seventhly, That there was nothing inferted in the Wednefday's paper, from which it had been fo unhandfomely excluded, of equal importance, or that was in any material degree deferving of the attention of its readers.

The Writer will not pretend to conjecture what powerful motives Mr. *Woodfall* could be fwayed by, after printing three parts of a work, and promifing the fourth, to refufe inferting the other two (efpecially as he had feen, by the Writer's notice to the Public, fuch was actually to be the extent of it) under fo frivolous, ungrounded and unwarrantable a pretence. It has, however, made him determine to publifh the whole at all events, in his own juftification, and for the fatisfaction of the public, though at an expence to the reader which he was defirous of preventing.

A

L E T T E R

T O T H E

Right Hon. Lord N O R T H, &c.

M Y L O R D,

WHENEVER meafures of high importance to this kingdom are under parliamentary confideration, it is the indifputable right of the people to exprefs their fentiments concerning them, either as collective, or corporate bodies, by inftructions, as conftituents to their reprefentatives, or by petition to either of the three branches of the Legiflature ; or elfe as individuals, by difquifitions or reprefentations from the prefs.

The times, my Lord, are becoming extremely critical from various alarming caufes ; and the attention, not only of this whole nation, but of the world, is awakened to what hath already happened, and may farther be expected. How far I may be encouraged to proceed, the experiment will only fhew. But at prefent I fhall exercife my right, on behalf

B   of

of my country, by pointing out some imperfections in the Bill at present before the House
of Commons " for the better regulation of
" the affairs of the East India Company," &c.
and I choose to address my remarks to your
Lordship on account of the responsibility of
the station which you occupy.

While it is my intention to represent boldly,
and with strength, I shall carefully endeavour
to avoid every appearance of cavil or disingenuity, and therefore my observations will not
be very numerous.

The tribunal proposed to be erected in India
is a supreme Court of Judicature, which is
" to have full power and authority to exercise
" all civil, criminal and ecclesiastical jurisdic
" tion by the new charter to be granted and
" committed to the said court; and also shall be
" at all times a court of record, in the name of a
" court of oyer and terminer, and gaol-delivery,
" and shall be a court of oyer and terminer, and
" gaol delivery, in and for the town of Calcutta,
" and factory of Fort William in Bengal, and
" other the factories and places subordinate, or
" hereafter to be subordinate thereto." From
the decisions of which court there lies no appeal
but to his Majesty in Council in England.

The jurisdiction, powers and authorities of
this Court are to extend to all the Company's
settlements, factories, subordinates and poffessions, now or at any time hereafter to be
acquired in the kingdoms or provinces of Ben-
gal, Bahar and Orissa; and to all British subjects and Christians who shall reside in the said

provinces under the protection of the Company. And the natives of India may likewife apply to the faid Court againft any of his Majefty's fubjects in India for any crimes or oppreffions whatfoever; to profecute any fuits or actions, real or perfonal; and alfo for any debt or complaint of native againft native, though the party fo purfued fhould be or have been in the fervice of the Company.

But on any complaint in writing being exhibited before the Prefident and Council of Fort William againft the Chief Juftice, or any or either of the Judges of the fupreme Court of Judicature, for mal-adminiftration of juftice, or any notorious or corrupt breach of duty or truft, then, after due notice being given to the accufed party or parties, the Governor and Council are to proceed to a hearing and determination of fuch complaints, and if unanimous in opinion thereon, they may fufpend thofe convicted, and appoint others to their offices; but the fufpended parties have a right to appeal, within a prefcribed time, to his Majefty in Council. All Chief Juftices and Judges, and all Prefidents and Counfellors, are likewife made amenable to his Majefty's Court of King's Bench on their return to England, for any breach of duty, or for any mifconduct or mifbehaviour in their offices or employments.

Such are the principal regulations intended for the new fupreme Court of Judicature in Bengal; on which the few following remarks are fubmitted to confideration.

First,

Firſt, It does not appear by the Bill, that this ſupreme Court of Judicature will have ſufficient power and authority to reſtrain the illegal and tyrannous acts of Governors and Councils, from whence all abuſes, oppreſſions and outrages have hitherto originated. The Governor and Council for the time being, in their executive department, or adminiſtration, are no other than the deputies of Directors, who are the ſervants of the Company, who are the deputies of the Sovereign, who is the adminiſtrator of every kind of ſovereign power in all countries that were acquired, or are poſſeſſed by any ſubjects of this realm; they therefore cannot in any thing be above thoſe laws which are executed by his authority, but muſt in all things be ſubject to them; as in executing his truſt they in no degree partake of his ſacred, impeccable, political character, which in its nature is incommunicable; therefore his ſovereign juſtice muſt neceſſarily be ſuperior in its operations to any other kind of power, eſpecially if exerciſed by ſuch as act under the authority of the delegates of his delegates. When conſidered in this light, it muſt appear an abſurdity to give an executive Board of Deputies, in a delegated truſt, a power to ſuſpend any or all of the Judges of a ſupreme Court of Judicature on exhibited complaints of the mal-adminiſtration of juſtice, without giving at the ſame time a power to the ſupreme Court of Judicature to ſuſpend a Governor, and any or all of the Council, on exhibited accuſations of injurious abuſes of

power

power that are tyrannous and oppreſſive; but more eſpecially as it muſt appear reaſonable to ſuppoſe, that the ſtations of the latter may be ably filled anew with greater facility than thoſe of the former. Thus will this Bill, if made a law, ſubject juſtice in India to a power which it ſhould controul, and ſecure that unbounded deſpotiſm to a Governor and Council which they have hitherto ſo much abuſed, though the contrary is pretended to be the great object in view.

Secondly, There does not appear to be any new reſource furniſhed for obtaining juſtice either againſt corrupt or wicked Judges, or oppreſſive Governors and Councils. Proſecutions in the Court of King's Bench, after their arrival in England, can only bring them to puniſhment; and thoſe have hitherto been experienced to prove ineffectual in many caſes of flagrant oppreſſion and injuſtice. Such proceſſes to parties muſt always prove extremely chargeable, and precarious in their iſſue, from the diſtance of places, the length of time, the influence of power in India, and the difficulty of producing proper evidence; none of which evils are propoſed to be removed by the Bill now depending in Parliament, not even by making written proofs, openly given and properly authenticated in India, to have all the force of *viva voce* evidence here, or to compel parties to come over and anſwer to charges exhibited againſt them. Till ſuch and other means for obtaining juſtice in England are furniſhed by law for injuſtice and injuries
that

that are fuffered in India, redreffes obtainable by law in England will be few and infignificant. There muft, therefore, be eftablifhed in India a judicial power effectual for the full punifhment of all kinds of offenders, or juftice will continue there to be more lame than fhe fhould be blind: all power will be grofsly abufed, and all protection but a mere farce. By the Bill now under confideration, the fupreme Court of Judicature is manifeftly fubjected to a more fupreme executive Board, which appears intended to be kept feated far above the reach of the laws of England in Bengal.

But, my Lord, it may be afked who are the perfons that fhould chiefly act in, or contribute moft to the bringing of offenders in India to juftice in Europe, but the Directors of the India Company, who not only act for their conftituents, but likewife in truft for the State? The Board of Directors, as deputies of the Company, and agents for Government, ought to be the profecutors in England of all who have been guilty of criminal practice in Bengal. But then fuch offenders will chiefly be their relations and friends; the very men who had been fent out to India and there preferred by them, and who durft only venture to act wickedly from a full reliance on their fupport, by the facrifice of honour, and to the violation of Juftice. Thefe are conclufions rationally drawn from the courfe of human practice, and which have already been but too frequently illuftrated by various ex-

amples,

amples, as well in the fcreening of guilt as the indulgence of malice, by rendering juftice ineffectual both for punifhment and redrefs.

In proof of the firft charge I appeal to the various cafes which we have feen publifhed of unwarrantable and illegal oppreffions and outrages that have been practifed; to the complainants of which the Directors have hitherto fhewn no kind of countenance, either by the punifhment of offenders, or redrefs of the injured; though in both of thofe meafures the good of the kingdom, the welfare of the Company, and their own honour, as men acting refponfibly in a ftation of high truft, were all equally concerned. Heavy charges of difobedience and guilt have even of late been eftablifhed at their very Board: yet hitherto no judicial proceedings thereon have been feen to take place, in fupport of their own violated authority, the honour of the Company, or the juftice of the kingdom.

I fhall now furnifh your Lordfhip with a ftriking inftance, from the proceedings of the very laft Board of Eaft India Directors, of the ftrong averfion thofe gentlemen are apt unguardedly to difcover to fuch innocent, injured men as apply to the juftice of this kingdom againft the outrages and oppreffions which they had been made to fuffer in Afia.

In the early part of laft year, as your Lordfhip cannot but know, his Majefty in Council was pleafed, by a folemn decree, to reftore Mr. Bolts to his ftation of Alderman, or Judge of the Mayor's Court of Calcutta, of which

he

he had been illegally deprived by the forcible
feizure and fudden tranfportation of his perfon
from Bengal to England, to the almoft entire
ruin of his own ample fortune, honourably
acquired, and with infinite injury done to the
concerns of many others that had been placed
in his hands.

During the procefs in England, which was
openly and regularly carried on, the Court of
Directors, nor any other party, ever once at-
tempted to vindicate the proceedings in India,
or to oppofe the relief fought by application
to the Throne for Juftice. His Majefty therefore, by the advice of his Privy Council, re-
placed Mr. Bolts in his office, and confequently
reftored to him the privileges annexed to the
ftation of a fervant to the Company in India:
on which Mr. Bolts applied to the Directors
for a paffage to be ordered for him to Bengal,
and was thereon informed, by their Secretary,
that a paffage would be ordered for him on
board a fpecified fhip; but if he returned
thither, he would not there be allowed to
carry on any trade.

My Lord, no other than merchants ever yet
did or could fill thofe ftations, becaufe the
annual income of a Judge of the Honourable
Mayor's Court is not fufficient to pay houfe-
rent for one month at Calcutta. An office,
therefore, for life in the Company's fervice
muft make the means of exifting in it a neceffary appendage; fo that the right of trading
was, in effect, virtually annexed to it, and had
ever been practifed. This inherent right Mr.
Bolts

Bolts did enjoy with that office, after he had quitted their commercial fervice by refignation, on account of repeated, partial and unjuft fuperceffions in preferment. He however held his poft of Alderman, and difcharged the duties of it with honour: and at the fame time, like the reft of his brother Judges, continued to profecute trade, to the great benefit of that country, the advantage of the Company, and the good of this kingdom; no merchant in that fettlement acquiring higher credit, or having fuperior fuccefs. After mentioning thefe particulars, it may be neceffary to inform your Lordfhip, that this letter is not written by Mr. Bolts, or by his defire or procurement, nor has the manufcript been fubmitted to his infpection.

Thus, my Lord, have the late India Directors, or at leaft the managing part of them, audaciously dared to defeat the juftice of their Sovereign in Council, the fupreme Court of Appeal from India to this kingdom, by rendering his folemn decree from his throne of juftice for the reftoration of a Judge to his office, becaufe illegally and unjuftly deprived of it, ineffectual and impotent; to the difhonour of the Crown, and with violation of the laws, by rendering fo facred an award of no effect; for a reftoration to office muft be fruitlefs, if the means of fubfifting in it are iniquitoufly taken away: and for which there could be no pretence grounded, but on fuch a diftinction as, in the opinion of every candid man, would difgrace even a gang of New-

C   gate

gate folicitors : for if he had, from fpirit and
a fenfe of honour upon ill-ufage, refigned his
commercial ftation under them, he continued
to occupy another of the higheft truft and importance; in the difcharge of which he only
could fubfift by the privilege and practice of
trade, which ever had been, and is to this
hour annexed to it in practice; nay, is what
he actually did enjoy to the very moment he
was unjuftly deprived of that office, and to
which of courfe he muft virtually have been
reftored with it by the folemn judicial decree
of his Majefty. Ponder, my Lord, on the
infult thus offered to your Sovereign in fuch a
horrid obftruction to national juftice, to the
violation of every principle of honour; and
then calmly confider if there is not fomething
neceffary to be done, highly worthy both of
legiflative and executive government, as well
for retribution to the injured as punifhment to
the guilty; one apparent great object at prefent to both being to eftablifh a permanent
fyftem of juftice in thofe very provinces, or
kingdoms, now appertaining to the Britifh
State, where fuch horrid outrages have been
committed on one hand, and fuch cruel injuries were fuffered on the other; and for the
redrefs of which latter, as now fhewn, even
Royal fupreme Juftice in England has here
daringly been rendered ineffectual.

My Lord, juftice can never any where be fo
effectually eftablifhed as by the making fevere
examples of fuch men as, for the ferving of
wicked purpofes, dare to violate, defeat, or
obftruct

obſtruct it. The object of India is become ſo intereſting to the people of this kingdom, that the attention of all men is now awakened to the meaſures in agitation concerning it. At many things of which they have heard or read, they feel high indignation; and they impatiently wait for the application of remedies that may prove efficacious for the prevention in future of ſuch oppreſſions and outrages as have been diſhonourable in government to ſuffer, and diſgraceful to human nature in practice. To the injuries Mr. Bolts has been made unjuſtly to groan under, the public has, perhaps, been beholden for his important informations, ſupported by ſuch authorities as have given them entire credit. The charges he has produced have not yet been anſwered; and, indeed, from their very natures they appear to be unanſwerable. Facts alledged that are falſe muſt be eaſily refutable; nor could there be wanting materials here for that purpoſe, had not his been irrefutable. Thoſe, therefore, who ſay his authorities will be diſproved, only mean thereby to deaden accuſations which they can by no other means evade. This, my Lord, is the language of the uninfluenced and honeſt part of the nation; and therefore not undeſerving even of the higheſt attention. And give me leave to remind your Lordſhip of a truth which you may rely on, that if juſtice for what is paſſed ſhould be wholly neglected, there will little reliance be placed on any meaſures that may be taken for prevention in future.

But

But to refume my fubject, and proceed in my obfervations on the Bill.

Thirdly, It does not appear upon the face of the Bill, that in the intended fupreme Court of Judicature either civil or criminal matters are to be decided by Juries, as there is no mention made of Juries but in the laft claufe or fection but two; and the whole of that claufe is as follows.

" And be it further enacted by the authority " aforefaid, that *any offence or offences com-* " *mitted againft* THIS ACT, or any of the " claufes, reftrictions, and regulations herein " contained, fhall and may be fued for and " profecuted, according to the nature of fuch " offence or offences, by any perfon or per- " fons whatfoever, in the faid fupreme Court " of Judicature to be by the faid charter " eftablifhed; in which no effoign, wager of " law, or protection, fhall be allowed; and " of all fines, by the faid " fupreme Court of Judicature inflicted and " impofed by the authority of this act, fhall be " to the ufe of the faid United Company, and " thereof to the perfon or " perfons who fhall profecute or fue for the " fame; *all which faid offences fhall be tried* in " the faid Court *by a Jury* of Britifh fubjects " refident at Calcutta, and not otherwife."

On the parts of this claufe that are printed in Italics and capitals, the following are the queries of a lawyer:

Query. Under thefe words what matters are triable by a Jury? And (Query) whether a
Jury

Jury can try any thing except what is charged to be an offence againſt this act?

Thus the Bill appears to want explanation. But I have been told by a Proprietor of India Stock, who has connections, I believe, with ſome Directors, that deciſions in the ſupreme Court of Judicature are not intended to be made by Juries. And as the juriſdiction of this Court is to extend throughout the three provinces, and only Calcutta Juries are mentioned in the quoted clauſe, we may rationally conclude, that deciſions in general are to be made by the Judges, without the intervention of Juries.

Hitherto criminal matters have been always decided by Juries, but others by Judges only. And we have lately had ſome ſtrange examples produced of judgments given by the latter in India.

My Lord, experience has ſerved every where to demonſtrate, and particularly under deſpotic governments, that reliance can very rarely be made on the integrity of Judges; who, to promote their own intereſts, will ſo interpret the laws as to make them anſwer any purpoſe; and no government can be more arbitrary than that of Bengal has been, and is likely to continue, for any thing we yet ſee to the contrary.

If your Lordſhip will examine the ſeveral applications heretofore made by India Directors for extending powers in matters of juſtice, and what uſes have been made of them, there would not need the inſtance juſt now produced,

of

of the Directors of laſt year even daring to render ineffectual his Majeſty's judicial decree, to convince you that they cannot be ſafely truſted with any influence over juſtice in India, which they certainly will acquire if judicial deciſions are left entirely to Judges.

Fourthly, The propriety, my Lord, of the prohibitory enactions reſpecting future Governors, or Preſidents and Councils, and the Chief Juſtices and Judges of the intended ſupreme Court of Judicature, muſt be too evident to be diſputed. They ought not, nor, as intended, are " to accept, receive, or take of or from
" any Indian princes or powers, or any perſon
" or perſons under their dominion, power,
" or authority, in any manner, or on any ac-
" count whatſoever, any preſent, gift, donation,
" gratuity or reward, pecuniary or otherwiſe;
" nor ſhall carry on, or be concerned in, or
" have any dealings or tranſactions by way of
" traffic or commerce of any kind whatſoever,
" either for his or their uſe, or for the benefit,
" profit, or advantage of any other perſon or
" perſons whatſoever, or of any foreign Com-
" pany in India, or by way of commiſſion for
" any foreign Company, (the trade and com-
" merce of the ſaid United Company only
" excepted); any law, uſage or cuſtom to the
" contrary thereof in any wiſe notwithſtand-
" ing :" and the oath propoſed to be taken by ſuch parties may be conſidered as a neceſſary and commendable precaution. The penalties, however, to be preſcribed for offences in theſe matters, ſhould be made ſufficiently ſevere; but
the

the provifionary claufe, which is inferted in
favour of fuch traders as fhall hereafter be
promoted to ftations of government, is too
vaguely and indeterminately worded for the
effectual prevention of collufive evafion. It
fhould be enacted, that on every fuch promotion
the party advanced in ftation fhall deliver in
to the proper officer of the fupreme Court of
Juftice a lift, upon oath, of all unconcluded
adventures, unfold commodities, and outftand-
ing debts, which lift fhould be regiftered for
the infpection of all men, in order that no new
bufinefs may be engaged in or carried on under
the colour of old dependencies, under large
penalties to be inflicted on principals, confe-
derates, agents, fervants, or dependents.

The claufe for regulating the rate of intereft
for money in India, if framed with due care,
may prove to much public advantage ; for
nothing can be more hurtful than a toleration
of the practice of ufury in a country of trade,
except the iffuing of fpurious money, and
forcing its currency in any degree, for that is
public robbery by the abufe of fupreme power.
The infamous inftance of tyrannical abufe in
the latter way that has been produced from
Bengal, and which was made a fource of
continual oppreffion and rapine to at leaft fome
of the then governing people there; and in
fact, in the firft inftance, the coinage was fuch
an abominable piece of roguery, as muft leave
every one concerned in it without the poffibi-
lity of excufe, becaufe it could only have been
the act of the whole governing body ; and
                                    befides

besides being contrary to the exprefs prefcriptions of the Company's charter, was likewife a moft daring offence againft the ftatute laws of this kingdom, it having been directed by repeated acts of parliament, that no coinages fhould be made in any of the Company's fettlements in India but according to the ftandards of the refpective countries. My Lord, public villainies of this kind muft be highly deferving of impeachments or indictments, as well for the due punifhment of criminals as *in terrorem* to evil-difpofed perfons, to intimidate them from engaging in fuch public robberies hereafter.

It muft be right to prohibit the receiving of any prefent, gift, donation, or reward, pecuniary or otherwife, from Indian powers, minifters, agents, or natives, by any of the Company's fervants, civil or military; becaufe, notwithftanding all that has been faid to the contrary, it is well known to be directly againft the very nature of thofe people to give any thing confequential but from compulfion, or for the ferving of fome important purpofe of their own. Every boaft made therefore of Eaftern generofity, from either pure friendfhip or gratitude, has been undeferving of credit. Such donations could not have been the effects of goodwill, but of menaces, extortions, or excited terrors; extravagant liberality being wellknown to be neither a virtue or vice of that country.

It is certainly proper, as propofed by this Bill, to prohibit the holding of any office, poft or employment, civil or military, under or by the authority of any ftate or power in the Eaft-Indies, either European or Indian, by Britifh fubjects. But I prefume to queftion if it is either conftitutional, juft or wife, to prohibit their going to, or refiding in fuch countries, if they are in a ftate of peace with us, in a merely trading way, though not in their military or marine fervice, or ftations of government; and while they do nothing contrary to the interefts of this kingdom, or repugnant to thofe of the Company : but in cafe of their doing either of thefe, they ought to be made anfwerable for fuch guilt to the juftice of their country. The fevereft punifhments fhould certainly be inflicted on all Britifh fubjects who are afliftant in fupplying either the native Indians or European foreigners in Afia with arms or ammunition of any kind, or for even dealing in fuch commodities without exprefs licence from the Company. But perfons refigning the Company's fervice from ill-ufage, or without guilt, or free merchants, free mariners, or any other perfons who go out with the Company's licence to fettle in India, fhould have a right to continue there as long as they may find it convenient fo to do, being made anfwerable to the juftice, and protected by the laws of their country ; nor ought they to be there fubjected to the arbitrary caprice or bafe malice of Governors and Councils in India, or to the partial views or wanton power of Directors in England, for being fuddenly ftopped fhort in their honeft purfuits ; perhaps from hatred of their merits, or envy of fuch

abilities,

abilities, as, without injury to the Company, their adverfaries may find are advancing their particular fortunes with the real interefts of this kingdom.

When men go from hence to fettle in India. they naturally relinquifh all profpects in Europe, but that of returning to enjoy the fortunes they may acquire; in doing which they act for the intereft of this country and the Company, as well as of themfelves. And wherever Englifh-men govern, and Englifh laws are eftablifhed, the juft and full protection of the latter is the equal right of all againft every fpecies of op-preffion or violence: and furely none can be greater than an unmerited arbitrary order to go, on a fudden, from one extreme part of the globe to the other. My Lord, it can be no other than damnable power, and diabolical juftice, to tear a man from all his profpects, perhaps, in a great degree, from all his pro-perty, and forcibly to tranfport him, without conviction of a crime. No government that is honeft will delegate 'fuch a power; and no men, but of the worft kind, would abufe it in practice. A man that is warranted to go from hence to India, goes thither now to the country of Englifhmen, and carries with him a right to the full protection of the laws of this kingdom. If his country can prove guilt on him there, or the Company injury, let him be fairly tried for either by a Jury of his peers, and be acquitted or convicted according to law: but let the law otherwife protect him from the punifhment of a felon, and not fuffer him, in a country that is fubject to his Sovereign, to be treated in fuch a manner as the Company cannot be authorifed to treat innocent aliens.

It muft be equally for the fecurity and profperity of thofe countries, and the advantage alike of the Company and this kingdom, that Britifh fubjects fhould be encouraged to fettle therein, not only for their defence, but likewife for the improvement of their commerce ; as no trade can be carried on between them and the other countries of Afia, but to their infinite benefit. Let, however, the European trade with them be confined to the European Com-panies, at leaft for the prefent ; but wifely leave that of Afia open to whomfoever will engage in it; as the fure confequences thereof muft be the ftreaming of great wealth into Bengal, of which England may avail herfelf for that moft neceffary of all purpofes, the retrieval of her circumftances; without which, her very fecurity, as well as her power, will henceforth be precarious.

Free traders of all countries, if not our na-tional enemies, or our rivals in Europe, fhould by every good means be encouraged not only to deal with, but alfo fettle in the provinces of Bengal, Bahar and Oriffa. They can carry on no trade without adding to the wealth of them ; and their refidence therein for the fecurity of their own property will naturally contribute much to the increafe of their ftrength. All men will act refolutely where they have pro-perty to defend, and interefts to preferve ; fuch

being

being the moſt powerful of all attachments, and the moſt ſtimulative of all incentives.

The articles which the India Company impoſe on their ſervants, or ſuch as go to ſettle in Aſia under their protection, of not availing themſelves of the laws of their country for redreſs for ſuffered violence or oppreſſion, or of being compellable to quit the country by force, after a year's notice had been given them to depart, though for no better aſſigned reaſon, than that it was not convenient for the Company they ſhould continue longer there, muſt in their very natures be illegal, becauſe highly unjuſt. No compact can be lawfully binding in which convenience is not reciprocal; and there muſt be implied in all a tie of indiſpenſable honour in the diſcharge of reſpective duties. No man who has not done a public or private injury ought, or conſtitutionally can be compellable to ſuffer any grievous puniſhment. Let not laws, therefore, be made to ſanction practical tyranny, or to deſtroy the rights of nature, the bulwarks of ſocial ſecurity and the very ends as well as eſſence of all compacts. While the Company had only forts to protect them for proſecuting trade in the countries of foreign princes, in regions very remote from their own country, there might at leaſt have been ſome colourable plea urged, from neceſſity, for ſtretching power a little beyond the conſtitutional line in ſupport of needful authority, and for the ſecurity of hazarded property in the hands of ſervants and dependents. But now, when thoſe diſtant

territories are annexed to the Britifh ftate, an
act to eftablifh the Englifh laws in thofe countries, to be adminiftered by an Englifh fupreme
Court of Judicature, fhould convey thither the
moft ample powers both for legal protection
and punifhment.

Any compacts that are not executable in
England, fhould not be fuffered to be executed
in the Bengal provinces: and I muft prefume
to fuppofe that no man can bind himfelf here
to fubmit to an arbitrary tranfportation at the
will, or for the convenience of any mafter or
patron, if he has done nothing to forfeit the
protection of the laws: and furely no one by
compact fhould be made tranfportable from
India to his prejudice, perhaps his ruin, without
at leaft the decifion of a Jury, that his conti-
nuance there would be greatly hurtful or dangerous; becaufe a contrary practice cannot be
Englifh juftice, but intolerable oppreffion, and
deteftable tyranny; fuch as would juftify re-
fiftance by every poffible means, even the moft
defperate that can be imagined, when pufhed
to the laft extremity. Indeed, my Lord, remote provinces muft be ruled by better principles of policy, or they can never flourifh,
nor will the poffeffion of them be fecure.

Fifthly, It cannot be deemed improper, that
any man in the Company's fervice, who fhall
be found guilty of extortion, breach of public
truft, embezzlement of public money or ftores;
or of defrauding the Company, or carrying on
any monopoly, after being duly convicted, and
the fentence of the Court in part inflicted,
fhould

fhould be fent over, or tranfported to England, if it be part of his fentence fo to fuffer.

But as in moft of the others, fo in the claufe now under confideration, (pages 11 and 12 of the printed Bill) there are great exceptions to be made to its contents in their prefent form, fome of which are as follow :

The claufe mentions conviction, by the judgment of any Court of Judicature, to be fufficient for warranting the Prefident and Council to immediately fend over fuch convict to England ; and moreover, that every fuch offender fhall be, and is hereby declared to be ———

Now the words *any Court* muft imply, that there actually will be more Courts for criminal judicature than one in Calcutta, which will have the power of inflicting fevere punifhments on Britifh fubjects, or other Europeans, for I muft fuppofe no Afiatics will be banifhed to this country : and as we know of no other criminal Court intended to be eftablifhed in Bengal, to which Britifh fubjects will be amenable for crimes, except that of a Quarter Seffions, to be held by the Governor and Council, as Juftices of the Peace; why fhould not the power of paffing fentences of tranfportation from India to England, be exprefsly confined to the fupreme Court of Judicature alone ?

The crimes mentioned in this claufe are of more than ordinary turpitude : and, as we may fuppofe, the punifhments to be inflicted on fuch offenders, will be fines and imprifonments in India, or fines and tranfportation to Europe :

an\

and as in the latter cafe efpecially it is reafonable to fuppofe, that fuch culprits will not be
the moſt infignificant of people; it may be
remarked, (and fhould be with refpect even to
beggars) that in all fuch caufes the Prefident
and Council will be profecutors, therefore parties, like the Sovereign in England; and by
their authority too, as by his Majefty's here,
the fentence pronounced on them will be carried into execution. Surely, then, the executive power there, any more than here, ought
not to be fuffered likewife to be the criminal
Judge; becaufe his fo being would make that
heterogeneous junction, or tyrannical monſter,
of Party, Judge and Executioner, whether
as an individual, or body of men; which cannot be conftitutional, becaufe deſtructive of
juftice, by the union of fuch powers as
would eftablifh a complete tyranny. And
furely, for perfecting juftice at fuch a diftance
from the feat of fupreme Government, it would
not be an improper precaution, exprefsly to
proportion the degrees of fines to the extents
of the frauds committed, or monies illicitly or
unlawfully acquired; and more efpecially when
annexed to the punifhment of banifhment, or
tranfportation from one extreme part of the
globe to the other.

In England Magiftrates hold Quarter Seffions, and can, and do inflict corporal and
other punifhments; fuch as light fines,
whipping, pillory, imprifonment, and even
tranfportation: but then, while the Sovereign,
by his deputies, is the profecutor and executor
of

of juftice, the parties accufed are always judged by their peers. Such, likewife, fhould invariably be made the practice in India; nor ought any but the moft perfectly conftitutional punifhments to be inflictable by the executive magiftracy at their Quarter Seffions in Calcutta. Thefe matters, therefore, are highly neceffary to be fully explained in the propofed act; and no opening left for Directors to fteal into the hands of thofe whom they may place in the executive truft in Bengal, any power to be fuch tyrants and oppreffors as they have been of late years, by the framing of fuch charters and laws of juftice as they hitherto have contrived to obtain. As to the blank left to be filled up at the end of this claufe, the Directors can only tell in what manner they wifh it to be done : but if they mean to extend any punifhment beyond the exprefs letter of the fentence, or act of tranfportation, farther than of difqualification for their future fervice, it moft probably is fuch as would be illegal.

Sixthly, Refpecting the claufe for prohibiting any releafement from, or compounding of debts, or penalties for crimes committed, on which judgment has been given in England or India, or for ftopping profecutions, fuits, or actions commenced for any kind of offences, I fhall only obferve, that if it does not extend to any kind of profecutions commenced after the punifhment of tranfportation had taken place, in confequence of a trial in India, it may not be improper. But if a perfon fentenced to pay a fine in India, has not effects there

to

to be feized for the difcharge of it, after he
had been tranfported to England, he ought not
to be made liable to profecution for it in this
country, nor for any thing elfe concerning
what he had been convicted of in Afia. All
juftice purfued in thofe regions ought to be
there effectually and finally compleated; or at
leaft fo far as to the very act of fending tranfports
away, by which the fentence will be there executed as far as can be done : even high treafon,
which has not been triable there yet, ought
in future fo to be. But with regard to penalties incurred from fuits or actions firft commenced here, there appears to be nothing ex-
ceptionable in the claufe.

Seventhly, The claufe for authorifing " the
" Prefident and Council of Fort William to
" make and iffue fuch rules, ordinances, and
" regulations for the good order and civil go-
" vernment of the faid United Company's
" fettlement at Fort William aforefaid, and
" other factories and places fubordinate, or to
" be fubordinate thereto, as fhall be deemed
" juft and reafonable, (fuch rules, ordinances,
" and regulations not being repugnant to the
" laws of this realm) and alfo impofe and levy
" all neceffary and reafonable impofts and
" duties on commerce and trade, for the fup-
" port of the faid United Company's civil
" government in Bengal, and to fet, impofe,
" inflict, and levy fines and forfeitures for the
" breach or non-obfervance , of fuch rules,
" ordinances, regulations, rates and duties;
" but neverthelefs the fame, or any of them,

E   " fhall

" ſhall not be valid, or of any force or effect,
" until the ſame ſhall be duly regiſtered in the
" ſaid ſupreme Court of Judicature, to be by
" the ſaid charter eſtabliſhed, with the con-
" ſent and approbation of the ſaid Court; and
" from and immediately after the regiſtering
" thereof, as aforeſaid, the ſame ſhall be good
" and valid in law : but nevertheleſs it ſhall
" be lawful for any perſon or perſons to appeal
" therefrom to his Majeſty, his heirs or ſuc-
" ceſſors, in Council in England, ſo as ſuch
" appeal, or notice thereof be lodged in the
" ſaid new Court of Judicature, within the
" ſpace of   days after the time of re-
" giſtering ſuch rules, ordinances, regulations,
" rates or duties : yet nevertheleſs, ſuch ap-
" peal ſhall not obſtruct, impede, or hinder
" the immediate execution of any rule, ordi-
" nance, regulation, rate or duty, ſo made
" and regiſtered as aforeſaid, until the ſame
" ſhall appear to have been quaſhed or vacated
" upon the hearing and determination of ſuch
" appeal."

On this compleat junction of legiſlative and
executive tyranny, the following obſervations,
made in order, are ſubmitted to the conſidera-
tion of your Lordſhip and the Public.

Hitherto the India Company, or rather the
Court of Proprietors, has been entruſted with
powers to make bye-laws, for regulating a
trade in which their own property was em-
barked, and for the good government of the
ſervants whom they had in their employ. But
by this clauſe it is propoſed to place an arbitrary

trary power, to be exercifed at will, in the hands of the deputies in India of the Company's deputies, the Directors in London, to make ordinances or laws, and to eftablifh fines and forfeitures for the non-obfervance of them; and likewife to impofe and levy fuch impofts and duties as *they fhall think neceffary and reafonable*, not only on Britifh fubjects in the fervice, or under the protection of the Company, but likewife on commerce and trade: which muft greatly affect fifteen millions of Indian people, now the fubjects of his Majefty, the people of other countries refident in any of thofe three provinces, all the countries of Afia, the factories, and, in effect, the commerce of other European nations, with whom embroils muft thereby be hazarded; and without any other check than the Judges of the fupreme Court of Juftice, who can, if they fo pleafe, refufe to admit their being regiftered.

These refpective powers, which are intended to be entrufted with the Executive Prefidential, and the Judiciary Boards, will have a natural tendency to eftablifh a common intereft between thofe parties which fhould act as ftrong checks on each other: and they, by co operation, may effectually purfue it to all lengths with impunity, unlefs the infliction of punifhments of every kind, but military, be reftricted to the fupreme Court of Judicature alone, and therein to be decided entirely by Juries. Nor can it be expected, with fuch powers in their hands, but that they will be continually feeking occafions for raifing money, even by the moft op-

preffive

preſſive means, for the ſake of advantages to be reaped from its expenditure. My Lord, temptations to colluſion ought effectually to be prevented, or they will prove deſtructive of all order and good government, and, in the event, ruinous to thoſe countries, the Company, and this kingdom. The power of laying on new taxes ſhould not even be entruſted with the Company itſelf, and much leſs with its ſub-ſtitutes, either in Europe or Aſia. The Moguls rarely exerciſed it there in the higheſt plenitude of their power: and all kinds of taxations upon a trade of exports in manufactures will, in their effects, every where prove fatal. They are ſo operating in England now, in conjunction with taxations by landlords, as your Lordſhip, the parliament, and the whole kingdom may readily ſee, by the prices of gold and ſilver bullion, the condition of the coinages, and the ſtate of real money among us : and they will much ſooner ruin India, (where a paper ſubſtitute will never do) if the Company's ſervants are there ſuffered to burthen the people as they pleaſe.

In many kinds of taxation, experience can only ſhew the effects of their operations: for which reaſon, and from conſidering the extents of thoſe provinces, it muſt be contrary to ſound policy, and the reverſe of true juſtice, to limit the rights of appeal to any number of days after the laying on of ſuch impoſts. Whenever taxes may be found indiſpenſibly neceſſary to be raiſed, all projected means for impoſing them ſhould be openly diſcuſſed in India,

in

in order that the objections which can be made, may be tranfmitted with them to England, for the confideration of the Court of Proprietors; which Court alone fhould have the power of making bye-laws, or eftablifhing taxations, under the infpection and controul of his Majefty in Council, if not of the Parliament, and with fuch concurrence only carried into execution. Laws ought not to be firft executed, or taxes levied in countries fo remote from the feat of fupreme government, and then confidered of here; becaufe fuch evils will be likely from thence to arife, as may afterwards be found beyond the reach of any remedies to remove.

Be extremely cautious, my Lord, of throwing unlimited powers into the hands of any kind of adventurers, in countries at fuch a diftance, whofe fixed object muft be the rapid acquifition of fortune. And who, in India, will dare to remonftrate againft any meafures of men that can inftantly effect their ruin by banifhment from the country, (if the executive and judicial powers act in confederacy, as the authorities propofed will not only enable, but likewife encourage them to do) unlefs protected by efficient laws in fo doing? The firft attention of fuch rulers, your Lordfhip may depend, will be how to make the utmoft they poffibly can, if left to the mercy and confcience of them for fo doing.

Having finifhed the obfervations I undertook to make on the Eaft-India Bill that is depending in parliament, I fhall now fubjoin fome
confiderations

considerations on the present state of the Bengal provinces, as likewise on that of the Company, and of this kingdom; and then conclude with some cursory remarks.

The unanswered public representations which have been made of the various illegal, oppressive and tyrannical powers that have been long exercised in Bengal, can require no farther confirmation than the very application of the Board of East-India Directors for a new charter of justice, to prevent them in future. Indeed, from the several allegations, charges, and proofs that have been produced, no rational doubt can be entertained of there having been horrid abuses and violences practised, as well in judicial proceedings, as by executive power in India; to the infinite wrong, not only of fifteen millions of defenceless natives, but likewise to numbers of traders and settlers of the countries of Asia, and many of his Majesty's European subjects. In short, the present state of those provinces is, that of great want of money, from the exhausting draughts which have been made from them by the Company and their servants, and by ill policy, in embarrassing, and in effect shutting up the many channels of Eastern trade, which used to pour abundance of wealth into those countries; a great depopulation, from the discouragement of industry by oppression; and a very powerful neighbour, watchful to reap every advantage from the effects of ill policy and bad government; with European rivals, made enemies from disgust, as well as by jealousy, who will be ready to

assist

affift in the accomplifhment of our deftruction on that quarter of the globe.

The Eaft-India Company, my Lord, were not inftituted for the governing of extenfive dominions, nor are they qualified for fo doing. They were incorporated for the fole purpofe of profecuting a fingle branch of national trade: and whether confidered in their legiflative or executive capacity, the degree of their real property in ftock, their fituations in the community, or by any fpecimens we have had of their principles or talents, they may certainly be pronounced unequal to the executing of fo important a truft. The known inftances of their not profecuting great offenders to juftice, and of their not granting redrefs to the moft cruelly injured ; but above all, the inftance produced by myfelf, of their daring even to render ineffectual their Sovereign's judicial decree, made in the fupreme Court of Appeal from India to this kingdom, for reftoring a Judge to his office, from which he had been illegally forced even into an unjuft banifhment, are, with the actual ftate of their affairs both in Afia and Europe, fuch proofs of their unworthinefs, as well as incapacity, as muft warrant our pronouncing them unequal to fo great a charge.

From the extraordinary changes that have happened in their affairs, the proprietary community have been made to fink into fubferviency to their executive fervants. By the extent of intrigue, the powers of combination, and the immenfely augmented means of gratification,

tification, both in India and in England, Directors, my Lord, have really become enabled
to be their own creators to, and likewife pro-
tectors in the arbitrary government of more
people than can be found in the whole Britifh
dominions that are under the immediate adminiftration of the Crown. They mayal moft
be confidered as the rivals of the Sovereign and
Parliament of this kingdom : and fhould they
continue in the courfe they are now purfuing,
with the increafing aid of imported wealthy
relations, dependents, and the means of corruption, they may bid fair in a fhort time to
be the makers of parliamentary majorities, and,
by degrees, alfo of parliaments ; nay, poffibly,
at laft, they may afpire at making Kings in
Europe as well as in Afia ; when, by the help
of their Hindoftan policy, they may, in effect,
make Leadenhall-ftreet the feat of fupreme
government over all the Britifh dominions on
every quarter of the globe.

It is impoffible, my Lord, in contemplating
on this fubject, not to recollect the power acquired in Italy, near two thoufand years ago,
by the Roman fpoilers of the Eaft, that inex-
hauftible fource of riches to conquerors from
the remoteft ages of which we read. And
though, in many things, the apprehenfions
that have been mentioned may be confidered
as extravagant, yet certainly many evils may
be dreaded, either from the mifapplication of
Indian wealth, or, in the prefent unprofperous
ftate of our other national trade in general,
from the unfortunate lofs of that fupply in
future,

future, by inattention or mifmanagement; for England may be made, in either way, to hazard wonderful difficulties, if not fudden ruin.

The ferious part of the people of this kingdom, from obferving how caufes operate, are already framing extraordinary opinions on the profpects of approaching times, as well from the unbounded power of corruption on one hand, as from a vifible extreme promptitude to venality and proftitution on the other, owing to the tafte and turn of our over-highly polifhed age. Soon after the revolution, my Lord, the refpective Directors of two different India Companies, with their own property only, found themfelves able to bribe King, Parliament, and in effect to coufin the whole nation, to grant and admit their acquiring two fuch charters as in their powers were incompatible with each other, and confequently in their exiftence illegal, though warranted by acts of parliament; and from law, as it was at leaft pretended, they derived effectual fupport. What then may not the joint efforts of thofe fince-united Companies hereafter accomplifh, with the power of plundering fifteen millions of people, added to the enormous profits of exclufive trade? Though partly painted in perfpective, the fore, or near ground of this picture, my Lord, is charged fufficiently with objects that are well worthy of attention.

This kingdom, with all its poffeffions, profpects and boafted ftate of profperity and happinefs, is unqueftionably in a dangerous,

F

an alarming fituation ; of which the following facts are indubitable proofs.

Our trade in exported manufactures, and efpecially for Europe, has fo very much decreafed, and therefrom the balances of trade have fo greatly turned againft us, that we are now in apparent want, and likely to be foon deftitute of real money in circulation.

The ftate of our coinages has become fuch, from the high rates of gold and filver bullion, owing to the decay of our trade of exports, that no filver coinages of his prefent Majefty have been made, at leaft none have appeared in circulation; nor, if they did, would they continue therein ; as great profits can be made by melting them down for fale as bullion, or for exports to pay debts or dividends on the continent. Gold coinages, as your Lordfhip muft know, cannot, likewife, be made but very greatly to lofs; the coinage price being three pounds feventeen fhillings and ten pence halfpenny an ounce, and the price of bullion at prefent four pounds and one fhilling. It has been a long time fluctuating between the rates of three pounds nineteen fhillings, and four pounds one fhilling and fix-pence. I dare then to afk your Lordfhip, the Bank Directors, and both Houfes of Parliament, if they are fkilled in fuch matters, if things can poffibly long continue to go on at this rate; or if they could have gone on to this time, but for the refources of Bengal? And thofe have been drained dry by one channel or another; info-
much,

much, that both thofe countries and thefe are now in great danger therefrom. No precautions of Bank Directors or of Government can prevent coin being carried out of the kingdom, while we have balances to pay; and all created difficulties or dangers will only ferve to increafe the quantities fo parted with. There is but one efficient remedy to cure the evil; which is that of taking care to have few balances to pay. This can only be done by lowering the prices of our manufactures, for procuring them fale at foreign markets. In order to do which, the land-rents of the kingdom muft be reduced to the ftandard they were at forty years ago; the farms re-divided, and their plundered rights of commonage reftored to the people. Ridiculous and impudent are the pleas of improvement, with public robberies, into national want and depopulation.

Sufficient proofs have been given of a great decreafe in the grofs number of the people : that of vagrant paupers is every where obvioufly augmenting, and parifh rates have been long growing enormoufly burthenfome. The people are driven by want to defperation at this very time, equally in England, in Scotland, and in Ireland; and there are now great defertions from all, but particularly the two latter countries. The act for regulating the prices of grain will have mifchievous effects. Its dam and its wier are a dream and a vifion : and the medium price it is defigned to eftablifh

is

is an eftimation of grofs ignorance, with refpect to the ordinary, or even extraordinary
prices of Europe: fo that, if the maintenance
of it is perfifted in, it will foon operate to the
deftruction of every yet-exifting manufactory
of the kingdom for exportation, and probably
bury your Lordfhip, with Mr. Arthur Young,
for ever under the ruins of your country.

Such, my Lord, is the actual condition at
prefent of this kingdom: and I dare your
Lordfhip, the Parliament, Bank, Royal Ex-
change, or the whole nation fairly to under-
take the difproval of it. There are, however,
undoubtedly wife meafures to be taken, that
would effectually operate for our national re-
demption; but I fear a want of honefty will
prevent their being adopted or purfued.

But farther, with regard to the India Bill,
in every light in which it can be viewed, the
appearance will be ftrong of its being calcu-
lated rather for the increafe than diminution
of defpotifm in Bengal. Unlefs all decifions
of importance are made by Juries, there will
no impartial juftice be adminiftered in thofe
countries: nor, without great freedom and
full fecurity in trade, can the Bengal provinces
ever again be made fo flourifhing as to be able
to enrich this kingdom by any other means
than the imported fortunes of fucceffive
fpoilers, oppreffors and tyrants.

It will be ill policy to permit the Company
to aim at engroffing the trade of Bengal even
with Europe, or to bury the revenues of thofe
                                        coun tries

countries in dead ftock at home; with ftrain-
ing their credit to make burthenfome impor-
tations, to the lofs of much intereft of money,
the increafe of expences, and at the rifk of
great injury from goods perifhing in ware-
houfes. Were the Afiatic and other commerce
more encouraged with thofe provinces, they
would foon abound with money; when, in-
ftead of over-imports of merchandize, the
Company might make moderate ones of bullion,
for the fupply of our markets, where it has
long been the fcarceft commodity known in
this kingdom.

It is a prevailing opinion, that government
cannot be entrufted with the adminiftration of
thofe provinces, though the right muft be the
fame as for thofe of America. I wave difcuffion
of the fubject; and am forry that government
appears in fo difgraceful a light. But with
regard to the interefts of thofe countries and
the Britifh ftate, the matter is certainly not
mended by leaving it in the hands of Eaft-India
Directors, for their fway is by corruption: and
the corruptions of Leadenhall-ftreet may,
perhaps, eafily be made auxiliaries to thofe in
higher places. But with regard to the fubjected Afiatics, and even the generality of Europeans, furely nothing can exceed the frauds,
iniquities and tyrannies of their double, let
me fay treble governments.

But if thofe unhappy countries muft continue farmed to the Company, with their
revenues of many millions, for what may be
confidered

confidered as a miferable quit-rent, the pre-
fervation of their poffeffion fhould at leaft be
confidered as an object of fuch importance to
the ftate, as to caufe a watchful eye, on the
part of government, to be kept fteadily fixed
on the conduct of thofe who are deputed to
rule them. I muft, therefore, prefume to
think, that it fhould be deemed needful for his
Majefty to have always a refident Minifter at
Calcutta, for furnifhing him with regular in-
formation of the ftate and profpect of affairs
in thofe countries; and likewife of the political
meafures of the Governor and Council, with
alfo the proceedings of the fupreme Court of
Judicature; in order that proper checks may
be timely given to all rifing abufes, and that the
whole machine of government may be fecured
againft deftruction from diforder.

The expence of fuch a refident Minifter in
India need not be made materially burthenfome
to government. His requifite qualifications
muft be competent underftanding, integrity,
and a confiderable knowledge of the interefts
and language of thofe countries. The poffeffing
of thefe latter muft make it neceffary that
he fhould previoufly have lived in Bengal,
either in the fervice, or under the protection
of the Company: and having been in fuch a
ftation, a moderate falary, with the privilege
of licit trade with the countries of Afia, but
anfwerable to juftice for engaging in any other,
would be a fufficient compenfation for the difcharge of his duty. He fhould, however,

have

have all the perfonal facrednefs and fecurity of
an Ambaffador ; and likewife a feat and vote
in all Councils affembled on matters of government and policy, but not in thofe for mere
trade.

Imagine not, my Lord, that I have been
propofing the inftitution of an office with the
leaft view to occupy it myfelf. I have not
addreffed you in the ftile of a fuitor; and,
having never been in India, cannot be qualified
for the employment. But I think policy,
honour and juftice may direct you at prefent to
the choice of a man, of whom the public will
perhaps be inclined to think more favourably
than of any other.

I am, with great refpect,

My Lord,

Your Lordfhip's moft obedient,

humble fervant,

****** *******